Yes You Can!

Yes You Can!

"I always get to where I am going by leaving behind where I have been" - J.T.R.

Published by Furry Thong Futritt, Portugal. 2022.

Cover by JTR

Joseph T. Riach

NOVELS BY JOSEPH T.RIACH

Too Early For A Glass Of Wine?

and

* Coming Soon – New Mystery Thriller *

SUCCESSFUL LIVING

The Secret World Of Self-Employment

Mastering The Art Of Making Money

Winning Big In Life And Business

Self-Improvement Should Be Fun

The Simplest Sales Strategy

The Road To Joyful Living !

Because I Feel Like It !

Yes You Can !

All available in Paperback and Ebook formats at Amazon (.com and .co.uk), Barnes and Noble and other leading book stores.

YES YOU CAN!
Be Healthy, Wealthy And Wise

Joseph T.Riach

ISBN : 979-8844327193

© Joseph T.Riach 1998-2022 all rights reserved

All proprietory rights and interest in this publication shall be vested in Joseph T.Riach and all other rights including, but without limitation, patent, registered design, copyright, trademark and service mark, connected with recording this publication shall also be vested in Joseph T.Riach.

Joseph T. Riach

Inside Yes You Can!

ABOUT THE AUTHOR	1
FOREWORD	3

Healthy Attitudes

1. WHAT IS HEALTH?	7
2. A RATHER NASTY RASH	9
3. GOAL!	15
4. POLLY & THE BOSS	19
5. TRUE COLOURS	25
6. SMART ALEC SMART	29

Wealthy Ways

7. WHAT IS WEALTH?	35
8. THE TRICK TO MAKING MONEY	37
9. SO YOU WANT TO BE A MILLIONAIRE?	41
10. THE ART OF MAKING MONEY	45
11. MAKING MONEY MADE SIMPLE	55
12. THE MONEY GO-ROUND	61

Yes You Can!

Wise Moves

13. WHAT IS WISDOM?	67
14. MARK TWAIN	69
15. HAVE A LAUGH!	73
16. MAD!	77
17. PAL!	81
18. POOR MAN AT THE DOOR	89

Conclusion

19. ALEC SMART REVISITED	95
20. GETTING TO WHERE YOU ARE GOING	103
21. THE MASTER MOVES	107
END WORD	111
REFERENCES AND RESOURCES	113
COPYRIGHT AND DISCLAIMER	117

Joseph T. Riach

ABOUT THE AUTHOR

Joseph Tom Riach is an entrepreneur and business adviser from the Scottish city of Aberdeen. He attended the city's famous Grammar School (as had Lord Byron in a previous era) and it was there he first developed a penchant for writing.

As both a lifelong fitness fanatic and as the owner of, and consultant to, a host of companies and businesses operating in every conceivable sector, Tom can certainly lay claim to knowing more than just a thing or two about health and the creation of wealth.

As regards wisdom? He'll let you be the judge of that.

But his lifetime of experience as an independent spirit and boss of his own destiny has led him to very definite conclusions about successful living which he shares with readers in his highly acclaimed series of books on the subject.

Tom not only writes about personal achievement, he writes novels too. He works from his long-time home in the sunny south of Portugal.

Joseph T. Riach

FOREWORD

"Early To Bed, Early To Rise, Makes You Healthy, Wealthy And Wise!"

There's a lot of truth in the old *'early to bed and early to rise'* saying but in this book I'm putting aside the 'bedding and rising' part and concentrating on just Health, Wealth and Wisdom. With these three aspects of your being in good working order, then your life generally is best set to be the fun and exciting adventure it should be.

Nevertheless, a healthy lifestyle depends on exercise, nutrition - and good rest. So getting the right amount of sleep, at the right times, is certainly a good starting point to all round well-being.

Good sleep refreshes both the body and the mind. Avoiding too many late nights and rising early provides tranquil hours of calm to plan and start your day with a fresh mind full of ideas and a relaxed body bursting with energy.

Many great achievers, and people of all persuasions, attest to the fact that they produce their best work and get most done in those early hours when other folk are still asleep. As an author it certainly works for me!

So here I am, bright and early, writing three sections of short articles under the headings of Health, Wealth and Wisdom which I hope will enlighten and entertain you. Each of the fifteen story chapters introduces you to one of my all-time **Master Moves** *for success in life.*

The stories are written in a light vein, easy reading, but meaningful too. My hope is that their message packs a punch. Not a knock-out blow of course but a gentle rap sufficient to raise you from slumber and set you on your way to a healthy, wealthy and wise new day.

HEALTHY ATTITUDES

"The only way to keep your health is to eat what you don't want, drink what you don't like, and do what you'd rather not." - Mark Twain

Joseph T. Riach

Chapter 1

WHAT IS HEALTH

"Life is short, break the rules and never forget anything that makes you smile!" - Mark Twain

What defines health? What makes you healthy? There are many different answers. Some folks might point to luck or family history, others to personal lifestyle. But there's generally a bit more to good health than that. My simple definition of health is - *'a state of complete physical, mental and social well-being driven by a positive attitude'*. I like to concentrate on the *attitude* aspect. To me attitude drives everything in life, including good (or bad) health.

You've heard of people being spoken of as 'having a healthy attitude'. This is not just a throw-away line. There is substance to the assertion. It refers to the individual in question as being upbeat, cheerful and optimistic; someone who sees opportunities where less 'healthy' folks see only difficulties.

Someone with a healthy attitude is likely to be adventurous, fun and generous, keen to forge ahead rather than dwelling on negatives. In short, they live life to the full and thrive whatever the obstacles; they don't give in because of them. Those of a happy disposition create good physical and spiritual health within themselves. On the other hand, people of a negative frame of mind make themselves unwell!

I can affirm that social, economic and environmental aspects of health matter greatly. They certainly do to me. I believe it's important that, in order to be healthy, you should be able to identify and to realise aspirations, satisfy needs and cope with (or where necessary transform) your environment. In this way health is a resource, an asset that helps you lead your everyday life. It's a positive concept and a reality which emphasises social and personal resources, as well as physical capacities.

Each of your experiences of health can differ widely and vary across your lifetime. But when faced with challenges, healthy attitudes provide you with the physical and emotional resilience you need to cope with situations, establish balance and live life fully.

Chapter 2

A RATHER NASTY RASH

How you feel about yourself is how others will perceive you. Those of a healthy mindset display their inner joy of being alive. On the other hand, nasty minded people are actually displaying their own inner loathing for themselves.

The latter group know full well that they are behaving badly but are unable to listen to their good voices (their conscience) instructing them to do better. Peer pressure plays a big part. Too many people have become victims, whiners, cheats with 'disadvantaged backgrounds', a sense of entitlement, mental anxiety and an expectation to be weak rather than a determination to be resilient and to get on with life and being a better person.

It is unfortunate but true that certain sections of modern society appear to suffer from a highly contagious and rather nasty rash, one of narcissism and intolerance.

Symptoms typically experienced by those infected range from mild displays of unkindness to others through to outright hostility. Sufferers show little regard for the sterling human qualities such as bravery, perseverance, self-sacrifice and community spirit of others but tend to celebrate weak-will and failure.

It seems that those who weep, wail and display personas akin to half-wits being devoured by flesh-eating aliens take prevalence over decent people who smile, take criticism with good grace, retain composure and have a proper idea of what is important in life. In short, those with a sense of perspective. But no, to such a reasonably balanced individual the reaction of rash-infected hysterics is often,

"Where is your victim-hood? Why are you not more miserable and aggrieved! You're not crying enough."

The trend is apparent in, to use a highly visible example, the world of professional football. As games are played in full public view and real time, they provide perfect insight.

As a life-long follower of the game, I played in my youth and dreamed of becoming a famous player. While I and my super-star heroes of the day were no angels on the field of play (nor off it), neither were we guilty of the petulant behaviour of present day players. All wanted to win of course but there was a certain code of acceptable conduct and no question of misplaced self-importance. Responsibility for win, loss or draw was accepted with reasonable grace ... the more so after time to cool down and enjoy a beer or two in the bar with opponents! All were in it for fun and glory – not for vindictiveness and self-pity.

Players and fans alike prided themselves on the quality of displaying a passion for the game in general, and for the team they followed in particular. It was largely well-meaning and harmless. Yet in current times has increasingly come to be characterised by blatant cheating, hurling obscenities at the opposition, match officials and even your own team.

Being professional, or a fan, has come to mean defending the indefensible when one of 'your' players misbehaves, and feigning outrage when a rival steps out of line. It means railing at perceived injustice week after week, while never acknowledging when 'your' team gets the rub of the green. It means earning thousands of pounds a week (players) or spending thousands of pounds a year (fans) for the right to be indescribably angry for two hours every week. And if you're not deeply unhappy - then you just don't care enough!

Passion or poison, that's the question. The fact is that when I look at players' and fans' behaviour, as at sectors of life in general, I can neither see nor believe that these people have anything to do with me, my ideals, my way of living. They don't represent my notions of fun, affiliation or sportsmanship. How can they be capable of such spite and malice over a mere game, a pursuit which fundamentally doesn't matter?

A supposedly entertaining diversion from life's drudgery has become the focal point for all their frustration and hatred. A sense of humour is seen as a sign of weakness. Fans and players seem motivated solely by negativity. A desire to see rivals suffer has overtaken the wish for their own team to do well. It's far worse than just a rather nasty rash!

Those who suffer from 'the rash' are basically insecure. They generally feel that their worlds are not under their own control. They perceive everyone but themselves as running their lives and having some degree of control over everything that they do. They subconsciously hand over the reins of their lives to another party. And they experience guilt where none exists.

At one time it was parental voices which mostly controlled and moulded lives. These were instructions and rules provided by authority, family and friends from whom core belief systems evolved. However, some external influences and people can re-engage that basic instinct for seeking parental acceptance. They do this simply by imposing doubt into your world. When you accept the guilt and self-doubt imposed by others, then you begin to live in someone else's context. You surrender your own belief systems and adopt those of the other party. In doing so, you begin to live by the rules and controls of the other person.

One area in which this occurs is in a professional or group setting where power and control are part of the environment. Politically savvy individuals take control of others by learning their ways, gaining their trust and then embedding doubt or a feeling of non-acceptance. In this way they impose themselves as the parental figure.

Over time, the subservient party grows to feel animosity towards their controller but is unsure why - other than for the fact that they don't like how they are treated. Once in this situation, it is difficult to break free of dependency on the controller and constantly seeking their acceptance.

Yet it needn't be so. The good news is that rashes, nasty or otherwise, can be cured. Better still is to live life in such ways as to minimise the risk of contracting them in the first place.

To do so means undoing the web of emotions and doubt that clouds your thinking. Go through your own psyche and find out which 'parental voices' are still present. Then dislodge them. Replace the old, worn out parental triggers with your own rules for living. Give rein to your own evolving belief systems. Don't sit and wait for acceptance from others. You'll wait a long time!

Make it happen yourself. Learn to accept yourself. You are the only person with a stake in your own decisions. You alone are responsible for your healthy, self-fulfilling life.

So, be it with football or life generally, conduct yourself with spirit and with good humour. It is perfectly possible to be competitive but compassionate too. Not at all a hard balance to strike and quite achievable. Work at winning while accepting that others have similar goals. Respect their dedication rather than deriding it. Then you can expect to enjoy some of the same consideration in return - and no nasty rash!

MASTER MOVE

"Establish yourself as the 'rose' in the room whose sweet fragrance drives away the 'rash' and draws others to you."

Joseph T. Riach

Chapter 3

GOAL!

Your team takes to the field of play. As soon as the whistle blows you launch into the attacking strategy which you have diligently prepared and practiced for in the weeks and months leading up to the game. In no time at all you descend on goal, you shoot - Goal! The ball is in the net and you rush to celebrate. But wait, there is silence all around. What is wrong? Slowly the truth dawns. First incredulity and then shame engulfs you. You have scored into the wrong goal. It's an utterly embarrassing own goal!

Improbable as the above scenario might seem, this is exactly what many people do in their real life affairs and businesses. They score 'own goals' with remarkable ease and regularity. Most often without realising that they are doing it.

How can this be? Let me explain.

These scorers of own goals I'm speaking of are neither incompetent nor lacking in self-determination. They know that setting targets, having goals in life, gives them purpose and is enjoyable. So they're on the right track - they're on the field of play and ready to score so to speak. They are prepared

to :
- Find motivation from within
- Take responsibility for their own actions
- Control their own behaviors and decisions
- Make decisions based on their own set of values

and
- Go for the goal that they have set themselves

but

Are they shooting for the right goal?

This last point is crucial. Because, just as on the football field where there are two goals, so in life there is a type of goal it is desirable to pursue and another not to. What if you have chosen to attack the wrong goal? In that case you will be expending all your energy on scoring own goals. So, what are the own goals to avoid? Here are the most common :

Putting money first

Chasing fame

Seeking status

Winning awards

Longing for admiration.

As your goals guide your behaviour and drive you to take certain actions, it should not be hard to see that setting your sights on these ambitions is hollow and short-sighted. They are motivated only by ephemeral outcomes of no substance. They are not the goals that successful 'strikers' aim at.

The top shots in life and business aim for different goals altogether. Their winning goals are :

Physical health
An authentic self
Community spirit
Good relationships
Personal development.

These goals originate from a personal desire or interest in something specific. The motivation is driven by enjoyment. Therefore their pursuit makes you happy because these goals can be directly fulfilled! They provide :

- Autonomy - Control of your own life, behaviours and destiny
- Competence - Mastery of tasks and skills which are personally important
- Relatedness - Being connected with real life, situations and the people in them.

So keep your eye on the ball. Choose carefully the goals you shoot for. Own goals are easy to score but hard to live down. You won't find what you really want from life through scoring them.

But when the ball hits the back of the net at the right end of the field, then the cry of, "Goal!" from your inner self and your supporters will tell you that your choice of goal to aim for was a game-winning and life-enhancing one. A goal to really celebrate.

MASTER MOVE

"Become the 'star striker' in life, with your eye on the ball and a nose for goal."

Joseph T. Riach

Chapter 4

POLLY & THE BOSS

The class had barely settled. The business studies students were still fidgeting into the cramped space of the small desk and chair combos in the lecture hall. Ignoring their general unreadiness, the lecturer's voice boomed out,

"Are you P.P.P.?"

That brought the class, myself included, to order. Now he had our attention.

"P.P.P.," he continued, "Prepared. Poised. Persuasive. When you display these qualities in your daily life and business you will be a highly effective individual. You will be healthy, bright and powerful.

Fail to incorporate proper preparation - such as doing your homework, mastering your subject, rehearsing your approach, knowing your contemporaries and clients, being aware of their wants, needs, personal preferences, foibles and characteristics - into your agenda and you will fail. Full stop.

On the other hand, assiduous attention to meticulous preparation will contribute to your self-confidence, assurance and all round presentation - your poise. A poised individual is calm, assertive and fully in control of all situations and the people in them. When poised you are impressive.

Which brings me to persuasive. Why persuasive? Do I mean that you should be compelling, credible and eloquent in dialogue? Yes I do, and very much so. But there is another dimension to persuasion which goes beyond just dialogue.

There is the persuasion of your presence. Call it charisma or star quality if you like. But those with whom you interact should sense it in you by your mere presence. The important thing is that others should instinctively trust you. And they'll trust you when your preparation and poise are apparent in your presentation.

So prepare yourself well and present to me for next week a short essay illustrating P.P.P. in practice."

I went home and gave his words considerable thought. Then this is what I wrote -

The 'Boss' enjoyed excellent relationships with those who worked with him. He cared for them in the same way that he wished to be treated. As such, there were few difficulties. But there was the odd exception ...

Polly, the factory workers' representative, was a petite young lady. Her dainty build concealed a hard-headed, tough as nails character more than capable of holding her own in most company. Short on size and experience she may have been but she called a spade a spade and spoke her mind fearlessly. Because of this, the Boss rather admired her. So he was not entirely unhappy when she burst her way unannounced into his office late one afternoon.

Without ceremony she launched into a hostile tirade

regarding the disparity in workers' wages between various workplace units. Particularly, she was displeased that assistants in the department where she worked earned ten pounds less per week than those in some other units. She demanded that 'her workers' be awarded a ten pounds per week rise and that all should thereby receive equal pay.

At face value this might seem to be a reasonable request. It didn't take into account however that the higher paid staff she referred to were better qualified and worked longer, unpaid hours when required. In short, she was not comparing like with like. Yet, despite the Boss politely pointing out this relevance to her, she persisted with her demand. She concluded by threatening to pull the workers out on strike if she did not get her way.

After some thought, the Boss informed her that he would indeed give 'her' workers a pay increase. Not the ten pounds per week she sought but rather a five pounds per week rise. At the same time, he proposed to reduce the higher paid staff's wages by five pounds per week; thereby establishing equality of earnings between all the employees - just as Polly wished.

Additionally, he informed her that he would notify those whose wages were being reduced that their drop in pay was her doing. He predicted that the disgruntled staff would soon remove her from her post of union representative and most likely see her dismissed from her employment too.

Polly became unusually subdued. Quite crestfallen in fact. She hadn't foreseen this turn of events. She didn't want to lose face by backing down. Neither, she realised, could she persist with her threats. The Boss let her contemplate her dilemma for some minutes and then, because he valued her spirit and recognised her talent, he offered her a 'way out' of her difficulty.

He asked her to consider becoming the manager of the unit in which she worked. Accepting this post would mean a substantial pay rise for her but she would of course have to give up her position of workers' representative. The Boss told her however that her management remit would include the responsibility of improving the quality of her workforce's output and increasing their productivity to the same standard as that of the other units. When she achieved this, then the workers' pay would rise accordingly. Everyone would win.

Polly's initial indignation at being out-manoeuvred in this way did not last long. She was smart enough to see the simple sense of the Boss's plan. She accepted.

She left his office with a quite different resolution to the situation than she had envisaged when she entered; but a highly satisfactory outcome nonetheless. Polly had also received a valuable lesson in how to evaluate situations with wile, a cool head and work out imaginatively beneficial solutions in a productive and convivial way.

She never knew of course, that the Boss's plan all along had been to move her 'onside' and into management. By waiting for the right circumstance to arise he achieved his objectives admirably. He allowed himself the briefest of smug grins, then headed to the pub for a celebratory beer.

When, on the following week, my effort was recognised as best in class, I did likewise!

MASTER MOVE

"Be prepared, poised and persuasive - the polished performer who does your homework, puts in the preparation, thinks ahead and earns respect."

Joseph T. Riach

Chapter 5

TRUE COLOURS

The expression *'True Colours'* dates back to the 1700s. It has a nautical origin and refers to the colour of the flag which every ship is required to fly at sea. Pirates used to deceive other ships by sailing under false flags so that they would not excite suspicion. The other ships' captains, thinking that the pirates were friendly, sailed their vessels close to those of the bandits and fell under their grip. It was only after their underhand approach and subsequent attack that the pirates would unfurl their skull and crossbones insignia thereby revealing their 'true colours'.

Your true colours therefore are your honest beliefs, thoughts, convictions, biases, desires; your real personality, character or disposition. To show your true colours is to demonstrate who you are and what you are really like rather than earning approval, trust and liking by pretending to be someone other than the real you.

It follows that people of integrity are open and honest about themselves and what they stand for in life. A description which, sad to say, cannot be applied with any regularity to certain groups in society. Foremost among the duplicitous are politicians. Most are patently dishonest and many are plain corrupt. If that is not the case, how do you explain the vast wealth which many accumulate throughout their careers while officially earning only a politician's salary?

The fact is that politicians are sponsored, their support paid for surreptitiously by international organisations, wealthy individuals, big industry, pressure groups, even foreign governments. Their ill-gotten gains are routed through a maze of concealed channels of course and sometimes plausible organisations; but one way or another they gain from the policies they enact from their positions of power.

Because of this, how you vote in a democratic election is largely meaningless. The true loyalties of your representatives of all persuasions lies with their paymasters, not with you. It wouldn't be so bad, but still pretty bad, if their interests were apparent; made clear to the public in the same way that sports stars and teams adorn their kit with their sponsors' logos. With them you know exactly who you are subsidising and what you'll get in return when you buy replica kit, pay to attend an event or subscribe to a pay-for-view channel.

Not so with politicians. They present themselves as 'Honest Joe', hide behind false promises and sell their souls to the highest bidder. Bidders who do not have your best interests at heart, only their own lust for wealth and power. These faceless entities are the ones who yield the real power in the world.

What I'd like to see is politicians show their true colours. It's not going to happen of course. But the next time you see a politician spouting forth with meaningless rhetoric, empty promises and feigned indignity, or government in process, bear in mind political commentator Jeremy Paxman's prophetic,

"Why is this bastard lying to me?" quote.

Picture if you will a scenario in which politicians do wear their sponsors' colours in the same way as football players and other sports stars. Imagine politicians' apparel festooned with company badges, their cars emblazoned with big tech and media logos, their place of work rechristened as the Amazon White House, the Google Westminster Houses of Parliamt or Number 10 Pfizer Street.

Viewed in this way, it is easy to deduce that the billions governments grant to commercial entities (pharmaceutical and armaments companies spring readily to mind), their support of these enterprises and their insistence that government procurement of their products, is not *'for your own good'* as claimed but is because they are being enriched through it. Their blatant corruption is surpassed only by their brazen denial of wrongdoing or of acting in any way other than for the common good.

But the good bit for you is that, once you implant in your mind the images which I have just drawn for you, you will never again look at, nor listen to, any politician with anything other than disbelief and total disdain. You'll smile a lot too! There are few things more hilarious than observing a fool at work; especially one who is fooling only themselves.

This is not to say that politicians are all stupid, far from it. But their lack of integrity is of an epic proportion. They should be the role model of no decent person. But they do serve the purpose of demonstrating how, as a decent person, you should *not* conduct yourself!

Don't live your life under 'false colours'. There's no future in that. You can deceive others but never yourself. Be upright and straight with people. Earn approval, trust and liking by simply being the real you; by being open and honest about yourself and what you stand for in life. Advance generosity, kindness and humour towards others. Do it with all people and whenever possible. Being of service to those less fortunate than yourself or in need in some way endows the most glorious sense of being of value. You are not being kind for reward, generous for plaudits nor funny to make yourself popular. You are doing it as a matter of choice.

Through it you will earn the respect and trust of others. They will recognise and value your integrity. What is the value of integrity? The value of your personal integrity is infinite. Sponsors' billions are but fools' gold.

MASTER MOVE
"Be one respected for your integrity and known for being open, honest and trustworthy - for always showing your true colours."

Chapter 6

SMART ALEC SMART

Alec Smart thought himself to be a rather intelligent fellow. Smug he was, but he worked hard too. So he found it particularly galling when he was payed off from his place of work. At first he thought that alternative employment would be easy for a clever and diligent person such as himself to find but, as the days passed into weeks and then the weeks became months, his optimism flagged. His lack of employment was getting him down. In fact it was driving him mad. Each day out of work had become a test of his sanity.

But every cloud has a silver lining. There's always tomorrow …

Smartly dressed, hair combed, tie straight and in good time, he arrived at the employment bureau for the work assessment interview. The receptionist politely informed him that the first part of the appraisal process would comprise of a spatial ability psychometric test. His confidence faltered when he found himself totally clueless as to what the heck she was talking about!

He was soon enlightened. She showed him into a tiny

room in which there was only a small table and chair. On the table was a board with nine different shaped holes. Beside the board there were nine different shaped blocks. There was also a pack of twenty cigarettes, a box of matches and an ash-tray.

The examiner arrived and told him that he had thirty minutes in which to place the nine different shaped blocks into the appropriate holes on the board. He blurted,

"Your time starts now!" and dashed from the room.

Alec sat down, picked up each of the blocks in turn and placed them into their matching holes on the board. With task completed and feeling both smug yet surprised at the ease of it all, he sat back to wait out the remaining twenty-nine minutes and forty-five seconds.

With nothing else to do, and although a non-smoker, he opened the pack of cigarettes, just out of curiosity. He withdrew one cigarette and again, just to pass the time, lit it up. It seemed like as good a time as any to try out smoking. He coughed and spluttered his way through the weed and stubbed out the butt in the ash-tray.

Then he took all the shapes out of their holes ... then put them back in again. Time was dragging so he lit up a second cigarette, smoked it, then stubbed it out in the ash-tray beside the remains of the first one. Then he repeated the pegs in/pegs out process and had another fag. He went through the routine over and over until he had taken the pegs in and out of their holes several dozen times and smoked all but one of the cigarettes. A thick fog filled the room.

Eventually Alec drew on the last cigarette and took all of the pegs out of their holes. He had just replaced the first of them into its space when the door of the room burst open.

"Stop!" commanded the examiner.

He looked at the board with just one peg in its hole, then to the ash-tray with its glut of discarded butts. He waved a hand at the choking smog, looked with pity at Alec's gray face, open tie and decidedly disheveled appearance. With a wry smile he gloated,

"Yes, it's a hell of a test!"

Some time later the examiner returned to the canteen where Alec was recovering over a much needed cup of tea.

"Good news," he announced, "One peg out of nine is not very good, but better than none. I'll give you a pass on the pegs. Congratulations!"

"Fabulous," Alec lied, as relieved as he was baffled. "So I have the job. When do I start?"

"Oh, you haven't got the job. No way. The position is only open to non-smokers. The work is in a fireworks factory!"

Kicking himself over his own stupidity and how easily he had been duped into disqualifying himself from the employment prospect, Alec retreated to a nearby pub. Consoling himself over a large whisky he reflected on the fact that his self-supposed intelligence, and work ethic too, counted for little. He realised for the first time in his life that what really mattered, and where he was clearly lacking, was to work smart! He needed to employ native wit, think clearly, read situations and see the bigger picture - and, he added, not as through a smokescreen!

"Yes," he concluded ruefully, "When I most needed to present myself as the real deal Alec Smart, I showed myself up to be nothing more than just another smart Alec!"

What's that about every (smoke) cloud and silver linings?

MASTER MOVE
"Work hard at working smart. Smart is much more than being educated or intelligent. It's about being aware - sometimes called street-wise."

WEALTHY WAYS

"Schools don't teach you how to be rich or how to be poor. They don't teach you anything worth knowing." - Neil Gaiman

Joseph T. Riach

Chapter 7

WHAT IS WEALTH?

Wealth to many people simply means having lots of money. That and the material possessions purchased with it. Many also feel that possessing money makes them important in society. In this shallow frame of mind they believe that others with money are 'important' too. So those who view wealth in this way tend to give more attention to those with money than to those without.

Look around you at the people in society whose voices are most loudly heard. The people that others listen to. You'll find that they are predominantly wealthy. Be they celebrities of some kind, politicians or whoever - they all possess financial wealth. It's their money, if you like, which gets them heard. Having money gives them power. Without money their power to be heard, to influence society would not exist.

Understand that - *Money can empower you. Money gets you listened to.*

Put simply, when you have money you possess the ability to influence people and circumstances in ways not possible when you have none.

It is also necessary to understand the simple fact that the

real power of money lies in having it ... not spending it. Spending it gives away that power. When you have it - hold on to it! Having it gives you choices not available to those without it.

In summary, having lots of money equals *'choice'* and *'power'* in your life. With those in play you can achieve and possess anything and everything - *of a material nature* - you might ever desire; and without spending any money!

But is that all that there is to wealth? Clearly not. Real wealth resides in your soul, your spirit, your being. It exists all around you in the natural world. Understanding those realities and living your life accordingly is to experience wealth in all its wondrous glory.

However, having money does give you more choice as to how you embrace the wealth of life, so having a good supply is no bad thing. In this section I'll show you exactly how to acquire it!

Chapter 8

THE TRICK TO MAKING MONEY

There is a trick to making money. You need one dollar/pound/euro to start with. Here is what you must do :

Put one dollar under a hat. Tap the hat three times with your magic wand and say the magic words – "I am wealthy". Lift the hat and voila! ... you will find that there are now two dollars.

Leave one dollar under the hat and put the other under a second hat. Repeat the magic process with that hat – tap it three times with your magic wand and say the magic words, "I am wealthy." Lift the hat and find that you now have two dollars there.

Leave one dollar under that hat and put the other dollar under a third hat. Repeat the process as before and then again and again until you have nine hats each with one dollar underneath them plus you have your original dollar to hand. You have now turned your one dollar into ten. Fantastic!

Now, split your nine dollars of gain into three pools of three dollars each.

Pool One is spending money – enjoy your profit and live a little!

Pool Two is to be saved - hold on to your new wealth. This is very important. The power of money lies in having it.

Pool Three is to create further growth

... so .....

Place those three dollars under a hat. Tap the hat three times with your magic wand, say the magic words, "I am wealthy," and voila! ... you will find that there are now six dollars under the hat! Now continue the process as before, placing three dollars of gain under successive hats until you have nine hats each with three dollars under them. That's twenty-seven dollars of gain. Plus your starting three dollars. That's thirty dollars – plus the three dollars spend and three dollars saved from the first round and of course your original one dollar. You now have thirty-seven dollars in total.

Add nine of these dollars to each of your spend and save pools. Add the starting three dollars to your original one dollar to create -

Pool Four – a fund for helping out less fortunate folks.

Next? You've guessed it – take the remaining nine dollars and repeat the nine hat sequence. With that sequence complete you'll have one hundred and twenty-eight dollars in total. Split it into the pools as before. Then keep on repeating the nine hat routine for as long as you feel inclined to or until you're sick of the sight of money (or hats) – whatever. This is the trick to making money.

Part of the 'magic' is that growth of the reinvested money accelerates exponentially through the power of compounding.

But, before you can benefit from compounding, you must first have cash to compound. For most folks that money must first be earned somehow. And to work profitably requires knowledge of your business, being excellent at what you do. That in turn takes learning, training and practice.

Therefore to perform the trick of making money, the sequence to follow is :

First : *Gain the knowledge to succeed – that's your magic hat.*

Second : *Work with excellence on your endeavour – that is your magic wand.*

Lastly : *Repeat the magic words, "I am wealthy," – that is programming your subconscious to make success inevitable.*

All of which leaves just one question. How to make the original one dollar into two dollars? It can be done in many ways and surprisingly easily. Are you ready to be a millionaire? …

MASTER MOVE
"Learn the magic formula of making money and employ it repetitively. Never stop."

Joseph T. Riach

Chapter 9

SO YOU WANT TO BE A MILLIONAIRE?

So you want to be a millionaire? Not unusual, many people harbour such a desire. Few however achieve their ambition. Most never get their dream beyond the realms of a fluffy fancy breezing around in their mind. In short they don't …

One : Evolve a concrete plan and …

Two : They don't write down their plan and …

Three : They don't act on the plan - which they never wrote down!

But, wait a mo …

… there's another infinitely bigger obstacle which blocks the way of those seeking millionaire status. Worse than having no clear idea of where to start, they are blind to one simple, yet critical factor. A reality essential to any aspiring millionaire but so obvious that it totally escapes their attention. What is it that they so spectacularly fail to see?

It's this -

$1m is One Million *ONE* Dollars!!

You want to be a millionaire? Then don't think millions.

Think One Single Dollar. It's only by knowing how to make $1 that you can accumulate great wealth. Put it this way - If you can't make just $1, how on earth do you expect to make millions of them? No chance! But, when you know how to make $1 then there is no limit to how often you can repeat the trick. Remember -

$1m is One Million *ONE* Dollars!!

Let's make that first dollar.

Find a solitary location with table and chair, quiet with no distractions. Put $1 on the table. Also a pen, a blank sheet of paper and a timer. Set the timer to 1 hour. Begin.

Draw a line down the middle of the paper, thus creating two equal columns. In the left hand column write how much money you intend to make (financial target), then how long you are giving yourself to reach the target (time limit). Eg $1m and 5 years.

Now, concentrate your gaze on the $1. As you do, think of and picture ways you can realistically turn that $1 into $2. As the ideas flood from your imagination, list them in the right hand column on your sheet of paper. Write down as many ways as possible to make just $1. When your timer sounds at the end of 1 hour – stop!

Now select your favourite way to make $1 from the list you've created, then immediately go out and put the strategy into practice – ACT NOW!

As soon as you have made that first $1, repeat the process. This time create $2 – either by $1 + $1 twice or by $2 into $4. Continue like this until your financial target is met – simple!

Yes You Can!

Pin your list in a prominent position where you will see it and be motivated by it each day. Use other strategies from your list as and when you consider it desirable. Add others as you think of them too.

Keep at it until you reach your goal. Determination and perseverence are all important.

So you want to be a millionaire? Then say, "Yes!" to One Million ONE Dollars!! It really is that simple.

MASTER MOVE
"Start small to grow big. If you can make one of something, you can make a million of them!"

Joseph T. Riach

Chapter 10

THE ART OF MAKING MONEY

Now that you've started to accumulate your *One Dollars,* you'll find that just about anybody will try to separate you from them! Whether it's friends, relatives, high street stores, online shops, travel companies, slick salespeople, banks or investment companies, all will try to 'get in on the action'. But it's not their action, it's yours. So don't advertise your wealth, keep your own counsel. Remember - when you make money – hold on to it! Don't listen to *Squander & Co.!*

Squander & Co., advisers to the financially inept, conduct their business from a shabby, downtown basement. Their depressingly squalid premise belies the fact that they have tens of millions of worldwide followers. These reckless zealots religiously adhere to Squander's corporate mantra of. "Spend, Spend, Spend!" This they accomplish with money they don't have and survive only on ever increasing credit. All the while Squander & Co. descend further into their own financial and moral black hole. As fine a place as any for the blind to lead the blind!

The fact is that a heck of a lot of you out there are

Squander & Company 'clients'. You squander money relentlessly. You often don't realise it of course (often you do)! but you are very easily parted from your cash. You are daily seduced with indecent ease by internet advertising, high street stores, smartphone offers, travel agents, credit companies, peer pressure and literally anyone who makes even a cursory effort to get at your money. You virtually beg to be relieved of it, competing one with the other in order to find the latest and fastest way of having it taken off you!

Here is something to try. Try to go through one whole day without spending a single cent. When you succeed, and it won't prove easy, try two consecutive days, then three and so on. You'll be surprised at how much spending you can eliminate when you really put your mind to it.

Try instead to concentrate any 'spending' only in areas that give you a higher return (more money back) than what you've spent. You'll then not really be spending anything at all. You'll be making money! Apply your thinking to your personal money management. On ways of only spending on bare necessities and on things which will earn you more money in return. When you do change your attitude you run the risk of becoming successful and wealthy. Squander & Co. will not love you for it!

So what of them? A board meeting was called in order to discuss their own dire situation. Half of the board members were 'too busy' elsewhere to bother attending. Those who did show were flippantly informed by the company accountant that he hadn't bothered to keep any records. Income and outgoings were as much a mystery to him as were sales records to the sales director and client records to the customer relations manager. He did however confirm there being cash available to finance lunch. So all adjourned to the local pub to discuss their next move.

This was soon determined as giving fabricated information to a dodgy lender for a sizable loan to tide them over until the next crisis. When this money arrived Squander & Co. moved into flashy west end accommodation they couldn't afford, purchased a company limousine they didn't need, went on foreign jollies to impress the gullible and generally 'spent-spent-spent' for no good reason at all. Soon they were back in their squalid downtown basement.

Does any of this sound familiar?

If so, you may wish to consider following the guidance of an altogether more prudent outfit …

Prosper & Co., advisers to savvy individuals, the self-employed and small business owners, work out of a pleasant office in a busy shopping precinct. The premise comes 'free' as part of a mutually beneficial arrangement with the mall company. Prosper & Co's significant base of regular clients pay reasonable fees, on a monthly in-advance basis, for a bespoke service particular to their needs.

Clients benefit from guidance centred on how modern society promotes in many people the tendency to act in haste and to act based on emotion. This is most clearly evident in buying and selling situations. What I call the *'must-have-it-now'* and the *'act-only-in-crisis'* syndromes. These two traits go a long way to explaining why the majority of ordinary people never get to be wealthy. They are squanderers. They squander time, relationships and opportunities just as recklessly as they waste money.

Prosper & Co's clients are, on the other hand, encouraged to be smart and opportunistic. They cannot become so by accident. They must employ wit and wiles beyond the scope of most others. This means that buying is only done with cash in hand, never in a rush and only in *'fire sale'* situations from *'act-only-in-crisis'* sellers.

When Prosper & Co. clients sell, they sell to the *'must-have-it-now'* mob, never in a hurry and always at top dollar. Most importantly they don't shell out their own cash. They use the sale of the goods or services to finance the purchase. The profits they accrue affords them quality time to spend on joyful living, fostering relationships and waiting for further opportunities. They learn that sooner or later the right opportunity will present itself. It always does.

These entrepreneurial types are both patient and smart. They cleverly choose to deal only in items both necessary and of quality. That way they know that there will always be a ready market. They also elect to involve themselves in a trade, profession or sector which gives them pleasure. A niche for which they have a real passion. This keeps them sharp in addition to providing a dependable source of income.

The key elements which Prosper & Co. urge their clients to employ and for you to take from their example are -

Realise *that labour, manual or mental, will never make you wealthy*

Trading, *buying and selling goods or services, is the smart way to prosper*

Trade *in something which excites you, which brings daily joy into your life* and

Never sell out of desperation nor buy on emotion. Do the exact opposite -

Buy from the desperate

and

Sell to the emotional. *Use them to finance your lifestyle.*

When you do then, just like Prosper & Co. and their clients, you are ready to become part of a prosperous world of opportunity in which everything is possible and failure is not an option.

When you do change your attitude and your mindset in this way, thinking and acting very simply and very clearly, then you run the risk of becoming the butt of others jokes and mindless comments. But you also risk becoming successful and wealthy. Which do you prefer?

Ask yourself -

How much do you know about the art of making money? Is it difficult?

Let's see.

I have money. You have something which I want. I give you my money for that something. Congratulations - You now have money!

Now here's something to think about.

How hard did you work or did you work at all in order to get that money?

Another thought.

Do you even have to be personally involved in the process in order to get my money?

One thing is for sure, it is not work alone which will determine how much money you make. It's possible for me to give you my money with no work on your part and even without your involvement in the process. How can this be?

I'll answer the question in five parts - but with some more questions for you too.

Okay, we agree that how hard you work really has limited or little to do with how much money you can have. The simple truth, amazingly missed by so many, is determined only by -

How many people like me give you money

How much I/they give you

and

What your profit margins are after you pay for any costs you accrue in the process.

See? Simple! So, the next key questions are -

How do you get lots of people to give you lots of money?

What do you give them in exchange that is so valuable that they'll keep giving you money, over and over again?

Thinking along those lines leads to the inevitable, and fascinating, realisation that there are only a very few ways of getting people to give you money (legally anyway)!

All you must do is choose one of the five alternatives listed below. They involve varying levels of 'pain' and labour for you, ranging from lots of grind to 'no sweat' at all! I've listed them in reverse priority. The inexperienced usually start out at stage 5. But with knowledge and experience anyone can progress through the stages, exceptionally even to stage 1 which is the ultimate objective and the top profit place to be. Here goes :

Method Five - Not so clever

Trade your labour, manual or mental, for money which your boss gives you and just expect that it will keep working. The reason this way sucks, is that you're intimately involved in the money-getting process, meaning that you have to show up to get paid. How much you can make is limited by the hours in the day and the magnanimity of your employer!

Method 4 - Smarter, but still not clever

Sell 'stuff' to people that they neither want nor need. This method can make you cash now but will cost you your reputation later. You're still intimately involved in the process and trapped, just like any employee. And, since people don't really want your product or service, you won't have any recurring purchases. It's a house of cards waiting to collapse!

Method 3 - Getting there, but not quite

Target a group of people who want something. Sell your product or service to them by leveraging what they want, to sell them what you want.

This method works well provided you know how to sell. And, when you have to convince people to do something that they don't quite want to do, you must always be coming up with inventive ways to persuade them. It is however, a viable and ethical way to sell valuable products and services to people who don't initially know they want them.

Method 2 - Almost the greatest money making approach

Source a product or service that a lot of people already want. Create the most effective and least cost way of delivering it to them. There's no real selling required. You can acquire customers, keep them longer and at less cost to yourself - provided you give great value. Plus, you can also up-sell them products that they don't know they need yet! This method leverages your customer base and is potentially highly profitable - and with limited work. But, if you stop working at it, your income stops.

Which leads us to …

Method 1 - The BEST way of all!

Do the same as at method 2 above but …

Provide an exclusive, high profit product or service, not available from anywhere else = **No competition!**

Sell into a specialised niche market of willing buyers = **Captive market!**

Set up a regular sale/up-sale/repeat sale and payment system = **Regular income, no involvement in the process on your part!**

The great thing about this method is that once established, people give you money without you doing anything! Now that's cool! Which means you can :

Do what you love

Make ridiculous income

Live anywhere in the world

Expend no energy, work or effort

… and …

Have money flow into your account on autopilot!

To reach this ideal scenario though, you have to get creative. You need a unique product or service. Think Gates,

Jobs, Bezos. Innovative thinkers, they invented (or adapted from others) their entrepreneurial solutions. However, you needn't be a technical genius to match their achievements. Great success is possible with modest ideas. I know, I've done it.

In my best-selling, *'Mastering The Art Of Making Money'* book, I give exact details of how to create and promote an exclusive product which sells easily with no input on my part. It involves no holding of stock nor physical movement of goods. No work after the initial creation in fact. The profit potential is limitless. I also reveal my ultimate *'More Money Less Effort'* strategy of creating wealth from just a few enjoyable hours input per week and with no product or service involved.

MASTER MOVE

"Work towards a minimum effort and maximum reward way of doing things. Buy from the desperate and sell to the emotional."

Joseph T. Riach

Chapter 11

MAKING MONEY MADE SIMPLE

Much is spoken of and written about investing and investments. What is good, what is bad? What is right, what is wrong? Stocks and shares, commodities, currencies, bonds, futures, gold, property, hard assets, cash? The list is endless, the possibilities too.

What is best for one person is worst for another. The right time for one, is the wrong time for others. The amount invested can be too big or too little. The objectives differ ... and so on and so on. The fact is that with so many variables there isn't a *'one size fits all or in all situations'* solution for investors looking to protect or grow their wealth.

Or is there?

While working as a financial consultant and business advisor I came up against these investment market questions, variables and situations on a daily basis. Analysis of clients' situations led to constantly changing, ever more complex and confusing (to both clients and myself)! recommendations. I longed for a simpler approach; a way to easily serve and satisfy my clients and reduce my burden too.

At that same time I was also employed as a creative

solutions specialist by both corporate and private clients in commerce and industry. This work involves devising approaches to situations within enterprises which overcome difficulties and/or improve any general or specific aspects of the businesses.

Success in this sector led me to thinking that, if I could come up with novel ways of resolving difficulties for these clients, could I not perhaps find an answer to the *'one size fits all'* conundrum of myself and my investment clients? I put my mind to work on that puzzle.

At first it seemed that I had set myself an impossible task. The financial markets are awash with possibilities and it occurred to me that the investment industry in general has little interest anyway in promoting one simple, universal solution. The big money for them lies in complex financial instruments and their own self-interest solutions.

So, in order to arrive at my conclusion, I started with three basic premises.

One – *the plan had to be simple.*

Two – *the plan had to be wholly effective.*

Three – *the plan had to be suitable for everyone.*

From there I went back to absolute basics. I knew that in the creation of solutions, the answer lies always in the question. It is necessary of course to ask the right question. I decided on two -

What *does every single person on the planet need and will always buy into?*

… and …

What *is the most fundamental example of investing in*

that way?

I came up with answer one – *Food!*

And answer two?

I reckoned that not many would wish to get their hands dirty directly involved in agriculture, livestock breeding or foodstuff manufacturing but they could invest in companies that did! I realised that by targeting reputable companies in the food and related sectors, buying their shares and holding them long term, my investors, whatever their objectives, could achieve their goals.

The fact is that the best quality, 'blue chip', high dividend yield stocks of top companies provide a remarkably safe haven, long term growth and regular income. All an investor must do is *buy their shares and hold them.* No trading or fancy dealing. As such, a portfolio of them can satisfy anyone's investment criteria – from short term income to long term retirement planning and all requirements in between.

I had found my *'one size fits all or in all situations'* solution for investors looking to protect or grow their wealth in a simple, sound way! So simple in fact that it had been staring me in the face all along. I had been just to darned clever to see it.

But when I saw how easy the strategy was to employ, how effective and efficient it was for all investors in all circumstances, how my reputation was enhanced, my responsibility reduced and my income increased, it cemented my belief that - **in all areas of life and business** - Simple Is Best, Simple Works!

~

Work in my investment business was stagnant. With little to do, I left my office and drove downtown. The hand-painted "Noah's Ark Investments" sign outside a slightly shabby shop front caught my eye. Intrigued, I parked up and went inside.

"How can I help you young fella?" came the hearty greeting from a ruddy-faced gent lolling in an old rocker. I kind of liked the 'young fella' line so immediately felt at home.

"What's with the Noah's Ark Investments?" I queried, "Is this an investment business?" - my face screwed up in puzzled mode.

"Oh it's an investment business alright my friend," came the assertive reply, "But not just any investment business. It is *the* investment business., the genuine article, the real McCoy. You see, what I do here came around long before you or any slick greenhorns saw the light of day and it'll be here long after you're pushin' up daisies."

"So what do you do?" I asked feeling well scolded, "And how come the odd name?"

"Nothin' odd about the name," he snapped back, "It says what it is. Clear and simple." Then, leaning forward he indicated that I sit on the threadbare recliner at his side and added, "Listen in an' you might learn something."

"Old Noah of biblical legend was no fool," he started, "When he filled up that boat of his with two of every animal, he knew just what he was doing. He was investing in his future. Think about it lad." Now I was a 'lad', even better! I eagerly leaned in to grasp the wisdom in prospect. It wasn't long in coming.

"In due course, each pair of animals reproduced. Then the offspring in turn did likewise. Soon he had herds of cattle and flocks of sheep. That was his capital growth." He paused to let the significance of that revelation sink in. Then he continued,

"Some calves, lambs, chickens etc. he slaughtered. These gave him food, clothes and shelter. That was his income. Those he didn't kill grew into the herd or flock. That was his reinvesting his profit, his futures market if you like. And so the cycle continued. When he required something outwith of his own production capability, he bought and payed for it with a lamb, calf or chicken. That was his spending money.

So you see son … " (wow, now I was his son, how could I not like this guy)!, " … Noah was the original investor. His methods are tried and tested. There is nothing new to learn about investing. All you need do is follow his example. Think about it. Noah neither attended Harvard nor wolved on Wall Street, he was much smarter than any of that."

Now my new friend beckoned to me and, with a conspiratorial wink, invited me to follow him. He led me to the back door and, throwing it open, revealed a back yard where gamboled several lambs, ducks and chickens.

"These are but a few, my full 'investment portfolio' is on the farm out of town," he laughed, "But I assure you young fella, good times and bad, they provide for my every need. More than that, what I do gives me, my family, my friends and my clients the greatest pleasure imaginable. Yes son, what I do is fun!"

"So you recommend these 'investments' to clients?" I asked slightly bemused.

"I surely do," he responded, "I recommend them, supply them and provide ongoing management advice. It's a full proactive portfolio management service. Yup," he slapped his thigh at that, "That's what I do," and let out a hearty laugh. I was deep in thought.

When I got back to my office some hours later, my PA was curious as to the cardboard cartons stacked in the back of my car. She was the more so incredulous when I explained it was my new investment portfolio and astounded when I showed her the rooster and six hens I had acquired.

Back home I built a wooden henhouse in the yard. Every day I collect the eggs, sometimes I roast a chicken. The flock grows with each hatch of chicklets. I sell some to fund my next investment - a piglet. The "Noah's Ark Investments" sign I put above the henhouse door attracts a steady stream of inquirers. My investment business is flourishing!

Easy teaser : Who is the legendary investor who, minus the actual farmyard, nonetheless employs the ultra simple Noah's Ark investment philosophy?

MASTER MOVE
"Know that simple is best, simple works. Stick to the basics. That is where great success resides."

Chapter 12

THE MONEY GO-ROUND

In this section on wealth I hope I have demonstrated how easy it is to make money - provided only that you approach the task with the right mindset. That is the big ask. You must see financial wealth for what it really is. Know that money can be a faithful servant but a tyrannical master. That is to say, there is nothing wrong with seeking material wealth but understand that the 'happiness' which you may believe it will bring you is largely an illusion. Real wealth resides within you. It is a state of being …

As the gleaming Mercedes limousine glided by, the garlic and pastis soaked old men playing boules in the late afternoon sunshine with the unemployed youths of sleepy Aucunes-Mouches-sur-Nous in deepest Languedoc didn't look up – but they Gallic shrugged anyway. The Mercedes drew to a halt at the aptly named Petit Loup, the town's run down XVI century inn, and Herr Geld-Taschen descended and entered the hostelry.

Renard the patron, hardly resplendent in his crumpled black suit, red threadbare trouser braces and smouldering remnant of a Disque Bleu dangling precariously from stubbled lips, welcomed the unexpected (and first for several months) visitor with barely concealed disdain and a surly grunt. But his demeanour transformed with remarkable agility to one of wide-eyed bon-hommerie when the German tycoon slapped a crisp five hundred euro note on to the reception desk and announced that he would inspect all of le Petit Loup's rooms before deciding in which one he would spend the night. Renard willingly handed all of the hotel keys to his newly acquired benefactor and directed him upstairs.

The instant the tourist disappeared from view, Renard grabbed the five hundred euro note and rushed next door to pay off his not inconsiderable debt to Monsieur Saucisse, the butcher.

Saucisse in turn raced down the street to Monsieur Sanglier the pig breeder who had been getting increasingly restless regarding the money due to him by the butcher on account of the money he himself owed to the Aucunes-Mouches-sur-Nous farmer's co-operative for several months worth of animal feed. So it was to there that Monsieur Sanglier now hurried to pay off his debt.

Very soon after the co-operative's receipt of this payment, Monsieur Droit, pillar of the community, Calvados afficionado and much trusted secretary of said co-operative, sneaked furtively via the back doors to the Douce Tentation bistro to pay off his burgeoning drinks account.

Madame Baisers at the bistro then only had to slide the money along the bar to Lolita the local whore who had also reluctantly been giving of her favours on credit due to 'pressure' from the town's Maire – none other than a certain

Monsieur Renard!

And it was to him at the Petit Loup that Lolita now ran to settle her room account.

Renard snatched the payment from her and had just relaid the five hundred euro note to its original place on the counter when Herr Geld-Taschen reappeared from upstairs. He declared himself underwhelmed by all the rooms of the inn and would not after all be staying there. He picked up his money and left.

Thereafter life in sleepy Aucunes-Mouches-sur-Nous returned to it's languid Langeudoc normality … but something remarkable had happened.

No-one had done anything, no-one had produced anything, no-one had earned anything. Yet an air of prosperity engulfed all. The whole village was out of debt and facing the future with renewed optimism!

Renard bought new trouser braces.

MASTER MOVE

"Know that wealth is a state of mind. Cash rich is largely an illusion."

Note : See translations of French terms at 'References and Resources'.

Joseph T. Riach

WISE MOVES

"Ridicule is man's most potent weapon. There is no defense. It's irrational. It's infuriating. It also works." - Saul Alinsky

Joseph T. Riach

Chapter 13

WHAT IS WISDOM?

Neil Gaiman famously said, "Schools don't teach you how to love somebody. They don't teach you how to be famous. They don't teach you how to be rich or how to be poor. They don't teach you how to walk away from someone you don't love any longer. They don't teach you how to know what's going on in someone else's mind. They don't teach you what to say to someone who's dying. They don't teach you anything worth knowing."

In short, schools don't teach *wisdom!*

But what is wisdom? A good question. For me it is an infinite treasure. It is - '*The ability to make conclusions based on the combination of knowledge and intuitive understanding*' or '*the result of applied theory and knowledge*'. You might call that - '*experience*', but I believe it's a lot more than that. Wisdom for me comes from learning principles and theory; testing those in practical application; assessing what is learned; then revising the theory and retesting the practical application accordingly and repeatedly; eventually, and only after prolonged intimate involvement, arriving at conclusions deemed to be '*wisdom*'.

As guidance for others, wisdom is often passed down in 'potted format' i.e. as short soundbites, mottoes and witty sayings. The last mentioned, humourous quips and one-liners, are universally popular. They are also among the most effective in conveying their message. Recipients relate easily to the often satirical content. The joke within the perceived truth of the text makes them memorable. Philosophers and writers recognised for their punchy, satirical style are seen as possessing great wisdom. This is often referred to as wit.

An outstanding exponent of the art of wit and wisdom, and my personal favourite in that respect, is Mark Twain.

So I'm devoting a chapter in this section to a selection of Mark Twain's most telling quotes. My own 'wisdom' is added to that by way of some short satires of politics, lawyers and authority in general. I hope you both enjoy and learn from them all.

Chapter 14

MARK TWAIN

I believe that wisdom is most effectively transmitted through wit. Especially dry humour and satire. It's the best way, people take note.

Mark Twain is master of the craft, renowned for his cutting edge humour. As an observer of life, commentator and critic of authority, his razor sharp humour is quite brilliant. I've learned much from his writing and frequently quote him in my own work. This because I see wit and wisdom as being the most natural of bedfellows. They complement each other perfectly and provide an easy and fun way of passing on my own experience to readers.

In his writing Twain honed a distinctive narrative style — friendly, funny, irreverent, often satirical and always eager to deflate the pretentious. By the age of just thirty-four years, the handsome, red-haired, affable, canny, egocentric and ambitious journalist and traveller had become one of the most popular and famous writers in America.

Mark Twain Quotes

Kindness is the language which the deaf can hear and the blind can see.

To be truly great, you have to be the kind of person who makes the others around you great.

Give every day the chance to be the most beautiful day of your life.

If we were meant to talk more than listen, we would have two mouths and one ear.

Worrying is like paying a debt you don't owe.

No amount of evidence will ever persuade an idiot.

I do love compliments, yet I'm often embarrassed to say what I think to the person when I get a compliment. I so often feel that they have not gone far enough.

Never argue with a fool, onlookers may not be able to tell the difference.

If you want to change the future, you must change what you're doing in the present.

Politicians and diapers must be changed often - and for the same reason.

When I was 17, my father was so stupid, I didn't want to be seen with him in public. When I was 24, I was amazed at how much the old man had learned in just 7 years.

It's better to be an optimist who is sometimes wrong than a pessimist who is always right

Good decisions come from experience. Experience comes from making bad decisions.

Nothing spoils a good story like the arrival of an eyewitness.

Why waste your money looking up your family tree? Just go into politics and your opponent will do it for you.

Yes You Can!

I was educated once - it took me years to get over it.

If voting made any difference they wouldn't let us do it.

Never argue with stupid people, they will drag you down to their level and then beat you with experience.

If you don't read the newspaper, you're uninformed. If you read the newspaper, you're misinformed.

How easy it is to make people believe a lie, and how hard it is to undo that work again!

Continuous improvement is better than delayed perfection.

The two most important days in your life are the day you are born and the day you find out why.

Never miss an opportunity to shut up.

Temper is what gets most people into trouble. Pride is what keeps them there.

Do not complain about growing old. It is a privilege denied to many.

Never allow someone to be your priority while allowing yourself to be their option.

Focus more on your desire than on your doubt, and your dream will take care of itself.

When you tell the truth, you don't have to remember anything.

If ignorance is bliss, why isn't the world happier?

They did not know it was impossible, so they did it.

Do the right thing. It will gratify some people and astonish the rest.

Censorship is telling a man that he can't have a steak just because a baby can't chew it.

Don't dream your life but live your dream.

There is nothing to be learned from the second kick of a mule.

Age is an issue of mind over matter. If you don't mind, it doesn't matter.

An open mind leaves a chance for someone to drop a worthwhile thought into it.

A little more kindness, A little less speed, A little more giving, A little less greed, A little more smile, A little less frown, A little less kicking, A man when he's down, A little more 'we', A little less 'I', A little more laugh, A little less cry, A little more flowers, On the pathway of life, And fewer on graves, At the end of the strife.

MASTER MOVE

"Know that some people get an education by not going to college and the rest get it after they leave college! But all get it by reading Mark Twain. Do likewise."

Chapter 15

HAVE A LAUGH

Good humour is a personal asset. It is a tonic for mind and body, lightens human burdens and is easily the best antidote for the anxiety and woes some seek to propagate in the world. Humour attracts and keeps friends. It is the direct route to serenity and contentment.

When you are happy you smile or laugh. It's the perfectly normal human expression of having your needs met, being entertained or simply feeling content and comfortable with life. Conversely, by consciously smiling, laughing or creating humour in your life you can make yourself feel lighter, more relaxed and at ease with yourself and those around you.

So it makes sense to make fun and enjoyment central to your existence, not a peripheral experience to fit in occasionally or when other activities or duties permit. Integrate the comedy into every minute and everything you do!

You will almost certainly have heard it said by someone, "I take my work seriously but never myself." Terrific advice. Such individuals are self-deprecating and generally their view of life is balanced. They know the importance of their trade or profession in creating material wealth and their responsibility to themselves and their families but understand also that they themselves are imperfect, flawed like the rest of us. They know their limitations and have learned, not only to live with their imperfections, but to laugh at them too. This is both wise and a fine example to follow. It removes the weight of others' expectations of them from them and releases them to work, to live, relaxed and effectively.

But when they say that 'They take their work seriously....' do not suppose for a moment that they don't take their sense of humour into their work too.

There are of course many of the daily activities of the work place which necessarily demand respect, reverence or solemnity, which need to be treated seriously ... and rightly so. None-the-less, all situations possess a funny side. The exposure of the mirth and humour inherent in them can actually ease the task in question, make it enjoyable for all and produce better results. People just become more relaxed, congenial and willing when in humour mode. When thus more at ease, they work better, more efficiently and more creatively. By having fun everyone wins!

As a teenager I was mischievous in the extreme, constantly in trouble with parents, teachers and authority – and ceaselessly laughing. Everything in life was a joke. In fact on the occasion of meeting up with a former classmate from school days some forty years on, my friend pondered on the fact that 'playing hooky' from school had not been among our regular misdemeanours and wondered why this had been so. The answer I told him was easy ... school was too much fun to miss! All those 'weird' teachers with strange names and hilarious mannerisms enabled us to 'take the mickey' all day long. Yes, school days were a blur of constant laughter.

Later I became more sober. As a young man making my way in life I felt pressured by sterner, more worldly peers to constrain my natural effervescence. With that I unwittingly lost much of the joy in life I had felt when younger. I had gone from the one extreme of over-exuberance, to the other extreme, repressed emotions.

The latter is not a healthy state of being but fortunately I emerged in due course from that into the realisation that nothing is gained from taking life too seriously … and in fact that a great deal is lost.

So I learned to integrate both diligence and humour into my daily life, work and being and it is in that state that I have truly prospered. I believe that I have grown in stature both intellectually and spiritually because my true nature is free to express itself without restraint. This I hope is amply displayed in my writing in which I combine serious dialogue with the comic and frivolous. It is a unique take on my subjects, but it is me!

I have spoken elsewhere about the art of writing and my feeling that the best texts depend on 'inspiration'. And that to be inspired I first need to have in mind to write about a subject about which I feel really passionate because, if I'm not, it will show in my writing. However, on a day to day basis, I have no idea if inspiration will come to me or not; and when it does come, what it is that I will feel inspired to write. What I do know is that I will write of a subject close to my heart, one which I know about and, more importantly, *feel* a lot about. Then my words will contain not only authority but will also *sparkle with emotion!*

More of the time than I care to admit (oh I am now admitting it)! my over-riding emotion is joy and what is in my mind is … fun and laughter! So that's what I write. I write all the crazy, hair-brained stuff which has poured from my mind since infancy. The nonsense liable to provoke concerned relatives to seek out institutions of secure accommodation for me! Mind you, Edward Lear gained fame and made a living from 'owls', 'pussy cats' and 'pea green boats', and the like. So there's hope for me!

Fun and enjoyment must be central to existence, not a peripheral experience to fit in occasionally or when other activities or duties permit. Integrate comedy into every minute and everything that you do! By consciously creating humour in your life you'll make yourself lighter of spirit, more relaxed and at ease with those around you. Watch the difference in the positive way they respond to you!

MASTER MOVE
"Set out every day to, first and foremost, have fun. Then build the rest of your day around it."

Chapter 16

MAD!

(Marriage, Alimony, Divorce)!

As I passed the fiddler on the corner screeching out the first few bars of his awful rendering of - "It's the same the whole world over, it's the poor what gets the blame … ", I dropped a couple of coins in his cap and crossed the road to my art gallery.

I prided myself on having located the business perfectly in one of those cobbled lanes in old London town which lure tourists like ladies of the night to Jack's ripper blade. Venturing into the gloom of the alley, the inquisitive would further be drawn by the scent and glow of the daily fresh-cut flowers adorning the gallery's outer entrance and from there to the dimly lit-by-carriage-lamps foyer exhibiting enticing miniature prints of Victorian street scenes.

Thence to the main studio with its high vaulted ceiling and massive oak rafters from which were slung art modern spotlights beaming on to full size portraits and landscapes in impressive gilt frames. In the gloomier alcoves and recesses various canvasses were randomly propped against the wall inviting the curious to explore. And on oil-paint spattered easels scattered throughout the exhibition a variety of apparently unfinished works were displayed, some half covered by dust sheets to give the impression of an artist just scurried off to a croque-monsieur and Bandol rosé rendezvous in a local bistro.

And chirping ever enthusiastically among the 'oohing-aahing' throng was my personal assistant Sherri, a petite bundle of blonde energy relieving the grocks (our derogatory name for tourists) of their holiday spending money with ease. I loved that girl's verve and charisma. She was worth her weight in Rembrandts to my enterprise; not that I had any of that or any other masters' works for sale. What I did have were quality works by genuinely talented local artists mixed in with 'Chinese art factory' reproductions, imported for peanuts and sold at massive mark ups. The grocks didn't know the difference.

Upstairs in the unused loft space my 'office' consisted of a second hand table and chair in a corner. My laptop travelled with me and there was a telephone. When it rang I answered politely as ever but my mood darkened when I heard Go Grabbit's voice on the line. Go was my solicitor.

"Have I got news for you dude!" exclaimed Go, "Do you want it good or bad?"

"Go on, cheer me up," I replied without enthusiasm.

"Well that smart little lady you call your wife visited me." Now he had my attention. "She showed me some photos and asked me if they were worth anything."

"You don't know anything about photos," I growled, yet he

carried on.

"Normally no, but these ones I recognised straight away and told her they were definitely worth four or five million pounds!"

"Wow!" I shouted, "That's fantastic! That's almost as much as my entire present wealth!"

"That's just what I thought," said Go, "Which brings me to the bad news. The photos are of you and Sherri!"

He hung up abruptly. I dropped my phone. The second hand chair collapsed when I slumped on to it.

From my position on the corner of the cobbled lane opposite my ex-wife's perfectly located art gallery, I could see that in the formerly unused loft space she had opened a private investigation service for suspicious spouses (P.I.S.S.S.) and in the gallery itself had added a photography section. The centre-piece exhibit in the latter was a photo series of exotic erotica featuring a naked couple and a labrynth of tangled limbs. The faces of the participants were in shadow but I recognised my miserable form and the curves of female buttock were unmistakably Sherri ... even in exile she was earning for the gallery.

And I was earning too ... well kind of. As I finished off my dreadful rendition - "... It's the rich what gets the pleasure, ain't it all a bloomin' shame", a passing grock dropped a fifty pence piece into my open violin case ... then took forty pence in change.

MASTER MOVE

"Create your own good fortune, appreciate it while you have

it and live so as to maximise the good things in life and minimise the risk of losing them!"

Chapter 17

PAL!

(Politicians, Authority, Lawyers)!

Veteran UK television current affairs commentator Jeremy Paxman famously said that he approached every political interview by asking himself,

"Why is this lying bastard lying to me?"

– but even the irascible Paxman never said it to a government minister's face live on air.

He did however tell the joke of bumping into an old school friend in the street one day and inquiring, as one does, as to what they were now doing. His friend replied that she was cooking food for mentally unstable folks with no grasp of reality.

Paxman assumed, "Is this charity work?"

"No," she replied, "I'm a chef in the canteen at the Westminster Houses of Parliament!"

~

My unscheduled scuffle with political pomposity transpired one tranquil afternoon as I dead-ended the joyful roses which bordered my lawn in the sleepy village, far from the chatter of the city and its hurly-burly officialdom, which I had chosen as home.

Lost as I was in my horticultural paradise, my mind fully engaged in pressing thoughts such as to the choice of Bordeaux or Bourgogne to accompany dinner and which glasses to serve it in, I did not hear the limousine pull up alongside where I pottered. I became aware of the intrusion only when the vehicle's passengers spilled out and their piercing jibber-jabber assailed my hearing. My initial reaction was that a bee, or a bevy of the buzzing beasties, had flown into my ear. They might as well have, the effect was the same. I jumped up as though stung.

Squinting into the mid-afternoon sunshine I could at first see only a pair of polished, patent brogues protruding beneath grey striped trouser bottoms, clearly of Savile Row origin.

"Dear god!" I thought, instantly conscious of my tatty garden garb, "What monstrosity of supposed civilisation has descended on me?"

My question was soon answered. The revelation turned out to be more ghastly than my worst fears. As my gaze travelled upwards I saw before me the unmistakeable bearing and the smarmy sneer of a … a … politician!

"Good day sir," came the introductory whine from the devil creature, "I am Horace Hornblower, your prospective parliamentary candidate in the up-coming by-election caused by the unfortunate demise of my esteemed colleague the Right Honourable Sir Willie Wang-King who, as you may be aware, sadly passed away when the hot air balloon he was preparing to travel in blew up."

Yes You Can!

The fact that a politician might disappear in a poof of his own hot air did not seem to strike Hornblower as even vaguely droll, so I restrained a smile and with feigned gravitas inquired,

"How dreadful, Lady Wang must be distraught?"

"Yes," sighed Horace, "She's looking forward to the acquittal!"

I chose to let that bombshell revelation pass without comment and quickly insisted,

"Look, I am terribly busy here but if you would like a cup of tea then … "

Before I could finish Hornblower cut me off in mid sentence and launched into full Honest Horace mode.

"I'm sorry," he bellowed, "But I can't keep shying away from difficult questions like this. People want us politicians to be up front with them and tell them the honest truth, even if it makes for uncomfortable hearing. And that is why I will never apologise for saying, 'Yes please, I would love a cup of tea', and if that upsets some people then so be it. I'd far rather be known for stating loud and clear to the whole world, be they at home with their families, at work with their colleagues or at play with their children that I am now and forever will be proud to say, 'Yes, I will have a cup of tea', than duck the issue and ignore my duty to the people I serve!"

I let him finish his faux pious diatribe before continuing very deliberately, "As I was saying … if you would like a cup of tea … then there's an excellent tea shop just along the road. I won't say that they'll be delighted to see you but … ," and here I faced him squarely and raised my voice, "I, sure as heck, will be thrilled to see you go!" With that I turned my back on him and returned to my rosebuds.

As Hornblower clambered back into his limousine and the attentions of his fawning entourage, I congratulated myself on having practiced the 'honesty is the best policy' principle of which politicians know very little. Lingering long into the summer evening with my soft-scented companions, I lived my regular reluctance to let my paradise day end. The old adage 'as honest as the day is long' came to mind. By that measure, politicians live very short days.

~

I took the half dozen eggs to the supermarket checkout and told the cashier that the woman behind me in the queue would pay for them. In the event this woman refused, citing the fact that she was in receipt of government welfare and therefore wasn't under law obliged to pay for my eggs - but she quickly pointed out that the gentleman behind her in line appeared to be in work and looked well off.

A quick interrogation of this man by security staff quickly established that he was indeed wealthy (ie worked hard and enjoyed the fruits of his own labour) so he was held down and physically restrained while payment for my eggs was extracted from him and the police were called.

He was arrested for having failed to voluntarily pay for my eggs while knowingly in possession of legally earned income and was subsequently found guilty of the offence; as a punishment for which the factory he owned (a place of gainful employment for more than 250 people) was razed to the ground, his house was confiscated and allocated to illegal immigrants, his car was crushed just for the hell of it, his wife was sold to a FIFA executive and his children taken to work on a drugs estate. I went home and boiled two eggs for my tea.

The next morning, being pay day at my place of work, I decided to put in my once per month appearance to pick up my 'entitlement'. I was on long term sick leave on account of an injured back which went in to spasm at any reference to the word 'work' and which seized up completely if confronted by an act of 'work' – but which was otherwise okay. On arrival I was appalled to find that the factory where I had been on sick leave from employment had been razed to the ground!

I went straight home and scrambled two eggs for lunch before banging off a letter of complaint to the government regarding the 'denial of my human right to screw sickness benefit from my employer'. I wrote a similar letter to the equal opportunities commission and, just for good measure, another to the organisation for racial and religious freedom. Lastly, I contacted a 'no-win-no-fee' compensation claim lawyer. Then I sat back and waited for the money to roll in.

On the following day I fried my two remaining eggs for breakfast and set off back to the supermarket.

~

With rapacious lawyers everywhere cashing in on the claims business by encouraging the populace to blame someone, anyone except themselves, for negligence (it used to be called an accident) with regard to even the most minor and ridiculous piece of misfortune, I decided that it was time for me too to get on the gravy train. But what to claim?

I first considered an action against my local baker for

selling me bread which turned brown when toasted. Then I thought to make a claim against the toaster manufacturer themselves for selling a product which not only scorched my bread but also electrocuted me whenever I put my hand into it while standing barefoot in a basin of salted water.

But eventually I decided on a simpler route, a claim against my lawyer himself. One for mental anguish and loss of windfall profit caused by his failure to initiate any spurious claim for damages on my behalf while knowingly in possession of the capability to do so! So I telephoned my lawyers.

"Lister, Lister and Lister," answered the superior male voice, "How may I be of assistance?"

"I'd like to speak to Mr.Lister," I said.

"That won't be possible sir. Mr.Lister is conducting the defense in a case of most serious criminal significance at the High Court and will be fully engaged there for several weeks. Is there anything else I can do for you?"

"Well in that case, can I speak to Mr.Lister?" slightly non-plussed.

"I'm very sorry sir, that won't be possible. Mr.Lister is on annual leave, skiing in the Swiss Alps. He will not return until at least the end of the month, perhaps later. Naturally he cannot be contacted. Will that be all?"

"Not quite," annoyance evident, "Is it possible then to speak to Mr.Lister?!"

"Certainly sir, this is Mr.Lister. How may I help you?"

"Aaagghh!" I bit hard into my sleeve and stifled a scream. Then, summoning my composure and with appropriate

gravitas, I issued my formal instruction …
"Go sue yourself!"

MASTER MOVE
"Put your faith in yourself, fight for your freedoms. Governments, politicians, lawyers, mainstream media, big tech are not your friends. Realise this and act accordingly."

Joseph T. Riach

Chapter 18

POOR MAN AT THE DOOR

A destitute stranger came to my door. He asked for money. I gave him none but took him in out of the cold and fed him hot food and drink. I found a warm jacket for him and I sent him on his way with a copy of my *'Mastering The Art Of Making Money'* book. I suggested that he read it.

The following day, the same fellow returned to my house. This time he brought with him a wife and three children. Again he asked for money and clearly expected me to help him as previously. So I did. I gave him no money but took food and drinks out to them and some clothes and toys for the children too. I sent them on their way with a copy of my *'The Road To Joyful Living Book'* book and suggested that they read it.

On the third day the vagrant appeared again. This time with an expanded family of twelve adults and children. They asked for money and were somewhat aggressive in insisting that I help them. I gave them no money but did feed them soup and sandwiches in the driveway. They eventually left, albeit reluctantly, and I gave them a copy of my *'Winning Big*

In Life And Business' book which I suggested they should read.

The day after that, I was disturbed from my work by a commotion outside my house. When I went to investigate I found a crowd of fifty or more ruffians, led by the recipient of my goodwill of the previous days, jostling on the sidewalk outside my home They were shouting threateningly and waving placards bearing demands that I give them money, shelter and food. I called the police.

After the police had arrived, dispersed the rioters and taken the ringleader into custody, I went outside to clear up the litter left behind by the mob. Among the general debris of cigarette butts, booze bottles and human waste, I found … the tattered remains of my three books.

In reflecting on events later, I concluded that -

"If you give a man a fish he will eat for one day. If you teach a man to fish he will eat every day. But – a man who has no interest in, and no intention of, learning to fish will return for free fish every day until there are no fish left and the pond is destroyed."

Some months after these events, while engaged in writing *'Too Early For A Glass Of Wine?',* there came a knock at my door. I thought not to answer but, after some hesitation, relented and went to see who was calling. When I opened the door, there stood a scraggy young waif. He was clearly penniless and looked in need of a good meal. But, when he spoke, he requested neither money nor food. What he did say both pleased and surprised me.

"Can I read your books sir?" he pleaded, "I want to make

something of my life."

I held the door open and invited him in.

MASTER MOVE

"You help yourself best by helping others. But only help those who are prepared to help themselves."

Joseph T. Riach

CONCLUSION

"I always get to where I am going by leaving behind where I have been." - J.T.R.

Joseph T. Riach

Chapter 19

ALEC SMART REVISITED

You should know by now that success in life is just not possible without the application of single minded determination and simple hard work. The two are essential to any meaningful degree of achievement. Yet, there is another trait which, when added to the mix, raises you to a different level altogether, makes you unbeatable. To truly achieve happiness and tranquility and derive life's bounty of benefits to the full you must work smart!

In my earlier story of Alec Smart who, despite his intelligence and hard work, found himself to be no more than just a 'smart Alec', I sought to demonstrate that it is native wit which matters more than any other trait in achieving successful outcomes in life.

So – you must work hard yes, but work hard at working smart!

What is working smart? What does it mean? Well, as I see it there are three categories of work -

* Hard Work – Typically dealing with crises, pressing issues, deadlines, meetings and interruptions. Rushing around a lot and being very important.

* No Work – Attending to trivial matters, smartphone chatter, popular activities, shopping, games and time wasting. Procrastinating.

and

* **Smart Work** - Smart workers spend time on Preparation, Planning, Prevention, Relationship Building, Personal Development, Enjoying Life – AND - they employ their Native Wit!

There are in fact two distinct aspects to *working smart :*

Native Wit and **Life Practices**

Of the two, native wit is natural and devastatingly effective. Most people who are employing it didn't learn it. They do it intuitively, it's part of their character, of who they are and how they were raised. I see it more in country folk than in town dwellers. Those brought up to a rural way of life are more so required to be practical and live by their wits than their city cousins. Therefore they are more inclined to be astute in assessing people and situations. You can aspire to be like them and those others endowed with native wit by -

* Altering the way you think, your attitudes

and

* Consciously applying appropriate life practices

To do so you'll need to give consideration to the following. No smart worker has all of them, but the more elements you manage to include into your working strategy and style, the smarter the worker you will become :

Put yourself first

Yes You Can!

Think before you act
Know what you want
Ask for what you want
Control your emotions
Be innovative and bold
Be in the right businesses
Look on the bright side of life
Know and play to your strengths
Employ good life management skills
Employ good time management skills
Identify and act on the right opportunities
Create intellectual products and/or services
Provide a scarce resource into a high demand market
    Additionally you should -
Leverage other people's time and money
Hang out with only the best people
Know when to cut your losses
Keep things in perspective
Network and ask for help
Create and deliver value
Be nimble minded
Be Flexible
    and
Be generous, compassionate and kind!

Working smart means finding your strengths and knowing your weaknesses. It also means maintaining your personal integrity and never involving yourself in anything which diminishes you or goes against your personal values.

Above all else, working smart means knowing your self worth and never under-selling yourself intellectually or financially. Value yourself highly.

The idea of working smarter rather than working harder is not, of course, new. While it's easy to explain what working harder is – starting early, longer hours, staying late – it's far more difficult to define working smart. It is almost indefinable! It's an intangible entity, a state of mind, a way of thinking, a god given gift.

However, one thing is certain. Those endowed with native wit have an incredibly simple and intuitive way of seeing things. To put it the other way around, they do not see or recognise complexity in anything. They blank out complexity and are the smarter for it. *They are astoundingly quick at seeing the obvious.* They see what is in front of their eyes.

While working hard entails much work, it is work which is not necessarily going to make a lot of difference. Smart work on the other hand makes a substantially bigger and far speedier, impact.

To work smart :

* Focus on only those things which actually move you forward in life.

* Separate out mundane tasks. Let others do them.

* Create disciplined but fun schedules with regular breaks.

* Do the hardest things first and early in the morning while your brain is fresh and alert.

* Don't procrastinate or do tasks only partially. Start them *now* and see them through to completion.

* Be selective about doing only genuinely high pay-off activities.

* Plan your activities ahead, rehearse as necessary.

* Remember too that enthusiasm should be tempered with wisdom. Consider beforehand, and at your leisure, all the details of whatever it is that you are contemplating so you can be sure that everything will be accomplished without fuss, on time and accurately.

* At the point of involvement, focus on fun elements and enjoying what you are doing.

* Avoid complex situations and people. Sticking to simple works.

* Work out ways to make life tasks easier or delegate them to others.

* *The importance of 'No'.* There is no single ability which constitutes working smart than saying *"No"* when you need to.

Whether in personal life or in business, there is no benefit in taking on un-necessary work, allowing others to be unrealistic in their expectations of you or simply having people take advantage of your good nature. In order to dedicate yourself to the important aspects of your life or business you must know when to say, and be confident in saying, "No," to things which contribute nothing to your well-being or to the achievement of your objectives. Practice by saying "No" to as many people as possible, as often as possible. Do it just for the hell of it! You'll feel great. Saying 'No' is saying 'Yes' to owning your own future.

In reality, not just this chapter, but the entire content of all of my writings is about working smart. All of the guidance, suggestions and examples are about urging you to do just that; to dare to be different, to own your own future, to think and work smart.

The alternative is not appealing. It is to stay bogged down in the same rut as everyone else, as all those who are not daring to be different and are not determined to own their own futures. Where's the point or the excitement in that?

The main barrier to progressing as individuals and taking control of their lives which so many face is in their mindset, their attitude. When they encounter someone different to themselves, someone self-confident and in control, they become confused. They think that the difference is due to a freak of birth or some other cruel trick of nature to which they have been subjected. Therefore they look for the 'secrets' of the smart thinkers in ever more complex areas. Yet the very opposite is the truth.

Those who work smart generally follow very simple life practices. So simple in fact that the majority of people cannot see or will not believe that these practices are at the very heart of the smart thinkers' existence.

It's somewhat like the clue to the murder sitting on the mantelpiece. No-one expects it to be there, so no-one finds it. They search every nook and cranny, upturn every stone. To no avail. Yet all the time the answer is right there before their eyes. So with the art of working smart. It is simple activities carried out repetitively and well which mount up to great achievements.

Yet this is what so many cannot or will not see. Before you can become a master of the art of smart, it will be necessary for you to learn to think the way that smart thinkers do. This will usually involve a process of **uneducating** from your mind many well entrenched beliefs and practices.

As very young children we mostly all display a high level of native wit. A range of natural thought processes and actions designed to allow us to live successfully in the wild. Modern society sanitises out much of this through our culture and education. By the time most people reach their twenties, they have totally capitulated to the expectations of society and to the peer pressure of the majority. They are thinking and acting just like the rest of the population who display, in all their thoughts and actions, a desperate desire to be equal in mediocrity. Don't let this be you!

Make it your aim to tap into the reservoir of native wit which still resides deep within you. Listen to your gut instinct. Work smart.

Joseph T. Riach

Chapter 20

GETTING TO WHERE YOU ARE GOING

I had been standing at the bus stop for what seemed like an eternity. It wasn't that there was any lack of busses arriving. A steady stream came and then left. All en-route to interesting, and some not so interesting, places. But none were headed for the destination which I had chosen; the location on which I had set my heart, where I dreamed of being.

I could have hopped on to any one of those busses which did pass through. Each one provided an opportunity to move on from where I was stationed and take me to somewhere new. And just going 'somewhere new' was certainly tempting. My ambition, after all, was to change my current circumstance for one with different horizons; a vista which would satisfy my growing ambition and sense of adventure.

But an opportunity is an opportunity and, with each passing bus, I was passing up on an option to pursue the change I sought. Any bus may not take me to my destination of preference but it would move me on from where I stood. That last factor was, I realised, the most important. Stagnation is self-fulfilling. So I changed tack.

I resolved to get on to the next bus that arrived regardless of where it was going to - but with one proviso. It could not be one going back in the direction from which I had come. Notwithstanding that, I reckoned that any destination which went some way to getting me towards my ideal location was a good move; a stepping stone to my future. From there I could then repeat the strategy, progressing in stages until I arrived where I most longed to be.

Thus decided, I looked forward with renewed enthusiasm for the next bus to arrive.

When it did, I leaped on board. Soon I was on my way. On my way where? I knew not. It didn't matter. Because, as I looked ahead at the unfolding view of the uncharted territory into which I was heading, I realised three things.

The first was that my destination, wherever it might be, was a surprise and a challenge in waiting. The arrival of the bus there would be both a thrilling climax to my journey and the opening of a new and exciting chapter in my life.

The second thing was that I determined to enjoy the journey. I sat back, relaxed and took in everything and everybody around me. Soon I was engaged with new people and their lives, hopes and experiences as well as the changing countryside around us. I was already absorbing an expanded environment. I was living the moment.

But third and last, and most explosively, the fact hit me that the single most critical element in my day had been the moment of stepping from the sidewalk at the bus stop and on to the bus. As the bus pulled away from there with me on board, that was the point of change, my point of no return.

The days, weeks and months of prevarication, of thinking about change but doing nothing to enforce change; the hours waiting for the arrival of the bus to my perfect location - all were blown away in that one simple act of stepping on to the bus. It was the instant I came to learn what I now know :

Having goals (destinations) is essential to achieving outcomes

but

Outcomes are the result of actions

and

Actions must be instigated.

The hardest actions to take are based on tough decisions. Decisions which may necessitate moving on from familiar places, situations and relationships. Leaving these behind, rather than focusing on a particular destination, is what gets things moving. It's the moment that you 'step on to the bus' - any bus - that matters. After that, the rest is 'easy'.

I myself love new challenges. Arriving at hitherto unexplored destinations is thrilling - but - ***I always get to where I am going by leaving behind where I have been!*** Knowing that is the key to getting to where you are going.

Joseph T. Riach

Chapter 21

THE MASTER MOVES

Here again are my **15 *Master Moves.*** Employ their guidance starting now. Stick diligently to practicing what they teach. Then experience the health, wealth and wisdom of my world grow within yours. Slowly at first then with ever greater momentum. A word of warning - Once started it's unstoppable!

"Establish yourself as the 'rose' in the room whose sweet fragrance drives away the 'rash' and draws others to you."

"Become the 'star striker' in life, with your eye on the ball and a nose for goal."

"Be prepared, poised and persuasive - the polished performer who does your homework, puts in the preparation, thinks ahead and earns respect."

"Be one respected for your integrity and known for being open, honest and trustworthy - for always showing your true colours."

"Work hard at working smart. Smart is much more than being educated or intelligent. It's about being aware -

sometimes called street-wise."

"Learn the magic formula of making money and employ it repetitively. Never stop."

"Start small to grow big. If you can make one of something, you can make a million of them!"

"Work towards a minimum effort and maximum reward way of doing things. Buy from the desperate and sell to the emotional."

"Know that simple is best, simple works. Stick to the basics. That is where great success resides."

"Know that wealth is a state of mind. Cash rich is largely an illusion."

"Know that some people get an education by not going to college and the rest get it after they leave college! But all get it by reading Mark Twain. Do likewise."

"Set out every day to, first and foremost, have fun. Then build the rest of your day around it."

"Create your own good fortune, appreciate it while you have it and live so as to maximise the good things in life and minimise the risk of losing them."

"Put your faith in yourself, fight for your freedoms. Know that governments, politicians, lawyers, mainstream media, big tech are not your friends. Realise this and act accordingly."

"Know that you help yourself best by helping others. But only help those who are prepared to help themselves."

On that last point, a final word. If you have enjoyed my work and feel you have gained from it, then please tell your friends, colleagues and acquaintances. Pass this book on to them. When they benefit from it I will be grateful and you will be the one who put the 'good news' their way. We all win. Very much a case of all that I write about, working in practice!

Joseph T. Riach

END WORD

"When a healthy attitude is absent, wealth is largely useless and wisdom cannot reveal itself." - Herophilos/JTR

I wrote this short book with two intentions.

First to afford you a brief introduction to me, my work and my series of *'personal achievement and successful living'* books and to my novels. I hope that your appetite is well whetted.

My second aim is to reveal just how easy it is for you to lead the healthy, wealthy and wise lifestyle which I champion. You should realise by now that success in living this way is down to just two things :

Attitude and ***Humour.***

Get those aspects right in your life, make them central to your being, and your existence will assume a brighter more brilliant hue. You'll exude an energy which not only drives your own endeavours but which radiates its warmth to all those around you. It is a universal solution.

That is why I hope that the book itself and the mood in which it is written, rather than just my words and stories within it, is a shining example of those qualities at play. If my texts inspire you to adopt a healthy mindset, and my wit and wisdom makes you smile and reflect, then for me it's *job done!*

Thank you for reading.

Joseph Tom Riach, Author

REFERENCES AND RESOURCES

Following is a glossary of people, places and terms referred to in *'Yes You Can!'*

Aberdeen - *East coast port and Scotland's third city.*

Aberdeen Grammar School - *Founded 1257. One of the oldest grammar schools in the UK.*

Ain't It All A Bloomin' Shame/It's The Same The Whole World Over - *Lines from the traditional lament, 'She Was Poor But She Was Honest. Author unknown.*

Saul Alinsky - *American community activist and political theorist. 1909-1972.*

Amazon - *North American e-commerce corporation.*

Jeff Bezos - *Entrepreneur and founder of Amazon Inc.*

Blue Chip Shares - *The most highly rated company shares listed on a stock market.*

Lord Byron - *Leading poet of the 'romantic' school. 1788-1824.*

Equal Opportunities Commission - *Statutory UK body formed 1n 1996.*

FIFA - *The international governing body of association*

football.

French - *Translations from 'Money Go-Round' at bottom of page.*

Neil Gaiman - *British author born 1960.*

Bill Gates - *American business magnate. Co-founder of Microsoft.*

Google - *Online services and software provider.*

Grock - *Swiss clown, composer, and musician known as 'the king of clowns'. 1880-1959.*

Herophilos - *Greek physician regarded as one of the earliest anatomists. 335-280 BC.*

High Court - *Usually the superior trial court of a jurisdiction.*

Jack The Ripper - *Notorious London serial murderer of the Victorian era.*

Steve Jobs - *American entrepreneur, industrial designer and co-founder of Apple Inc.*

Mercedes - *German luxury car manufacturer.*

Noah's Ark - *The vessel in the biblical Genesis flood narrative.*

Organisation For Racial And Religious Freedom - *Fictional entity of the author.*

Jeremy Paxman - *English broadcaster, journalist, author, and television presenter.*

Pfizer - *American multinational pharmaceutical and biotechnology corporation.*

Rembrandt - *Dutch master painter, considered one of the greatest visual artists in history. 1606-1669.*

Yes You Can!

Savile Row - *London street principally known for traditional bespoke men's tailoring.*

Swiss Alps - *The Alpine region of Switzerland.*

Mark Twain - *American author, humourist, entrepreneur and lecturer.*

French Terms in 'Money Go-Round'.

Aucunes-Mouches-sur-Nous - *No Flies On Us*

Boules - *Bowls*

Calvados - *Apple cider based brandy of France's Normandy region*

Disque Bleu - *French brand full strength cigarettes*

Douce Tentation - *Sweet Temptation*

Gallic Shrug - *Quintessentially French expression of disdain/disinterest (raised shoulders, tilted head, raised eyebrows, curled lower lip)!*

Herr Geld-Taschen - *Mr. Money Bags*

Languedoc - *Region in South of France*

Maire - *Mayor*

Petit Loup - *Little Wolf*

Madame Baisers - *Mrs. Kisses*

Monsieur Droit - *Mr. Upright*

Monsieur Renard - *Mr. Fox*

Monsieur Sanglier - *Mr. Wild Boer*

Monsieur Saucisse - *Mr. Sausage*

Pastis - *French aniseed-flavoured alcoholic spirit*

Joseph T. Riach

COPYRIGHT AND DISCLAIMER

YES YOU CAN!

BE HEALTHY, WEALTHY AND WISE
ISBN : 979-8844327193
© **Joseph T. Riach 1998 - 2022 all rights reserved**

All proprietary rights and interest in this publication shall be vested in Joseph T.Riach and all other rights including, but without limitation, patent, registered design, copyright, trademark and service mark, connected with this publication shall also be vested in Joseph T.Riach.

No part of this publication may be reproduced, stored in a retrieval system, or transmitted in any form or by any means, electronic, mechanical, photocopying, recording or otherwise, without the prior written permission of the copyright owner, Joseph T.Riach.

The right of Joseph T.Riach to be identified as the author of this work has been asserted in accordance with the Copyright, Designs and Patents Act 1988.

Designations used by companies to distinguish their products are often claimed as trademarks. All brand names and product names used in this book are trade names, service marks, trademarks or registered trademarks of their respective owners. The publisher is not associated with any product or vendor mentioned in this book.

Limit of liability/disclaimer of warranty. While the publisher and author have used their best efforts in preparing this book, they make no representations or warranties with respect to the accuracy or completeness of the contents of this book and specifically disclaim any implied warranties of merchantability or fitness for a particular purpose. It is sold on the understanding that the publisher is not engaged in rendering professional services and neither the publisher nor the author shall be liable for damages arising herefrom. If professional advice or other expert assistance is required, the services of a competent professional should be sought. This manuscript relates only the personal experience of the author.

This manuscript relates only the personal experience of the author. Where reference is made to equity options, crypto currency, stocks and shares and trading in these products, it is made only as a factual account of real experience. This book is not recommending that you do or do not use any specific trading system and readers considering participating in equity option or crypto currency trading are strongly advised to seek proper professional advice from an accredited stockbroker or investment advisor. The past performance of shares, equity options and crypto currencies are not necessarily indicative of future performance and the price of shares, equity options and crypto currencies can go in the opposite direction to that expected. No liability is accepted by the author or publisher or their servants or agents for the use by any readers of the information contained herein in any circumstance connected with actual trading or otherwise. The author is not a stockbroker nor investment adviser in terms of the Financial Services Act 1986 or otherwise and this book does not give any specific investment advice, it is not asking for investment funds, it is not inviting readers or offering to invite readers into any investment agreement directly or indirectly. The book is not advising readers on the merits of shares, equity options or crypto currencies nor is it advertising them and it is not inviting readers to buy or sell, or not to buy or sell, shares, equity options or crypto currencies. Whilst all reasonable care has been taken to ensure that the information contained in this publication is accurate and not misleading at the time of publication, neither the author, nor the publisher nor their servants nor agents, is responsible for any errors or omissions contained in this publication which is published for information only and does not constitute, or claim to constitute, investment advice.

Joseph T. Riach

Yes You Can!

'Yes You Can – Be Healthy, Wealthy And Wise' is available direct from the Amazon book store (amazon.com or amazon.co.uk) in Paperback and Ebook formats, Barnes and Noble and other leading book suppliers.

Receive notifications of my new books and novels as they become available, free and reduced price book offers and entry to periodic promotions for signed or personalised copies of my books, by visiting me at **www.tomriach.com** Click 'Contact' to leave a message.

Also, to help ensure that I can continue to create quality publications at affordable prices, I would really appreciate a review on Amazon. The number of reviews a book receives has a direct impact on how it sells, so just leaving a review, no matter how short, helps make it possible for me to continue writing books for you to enjoy.

To see a selection of the many reviews sent directly to me, but not featured on Amazon, visit my website at **www.tomriach.com** and click 'Reviews'.

Thank you once again for reading my work and for your ongoing support. Regards, Tom.

Author's Amazon Pages – *Joseph T. Riach*, https://www.amazon.com/-/e/B01MTQYSH3
https://www.amazon.co.uk/-/e/B01MTQYSH3

www.ingramcontent.com/pod-product-compliance
Lightning Source LLC
Chambersburg PA
CBHW050011230526
45465CB00003BB/1364